WORKBOOK

For

Trust

Knowing When to Give It, When to Withhold It, How to Earn It, and How to Fix It When It Gets Broken

[A Guide to Implementing Dr. Henry Cloud's Book]

Kelly Press

Table of Content

How To Use This Workbook

This workbook provides you with the chance to investigate a variety of aspects of your life, identify areas in need of improvement, and observe your advancement. It has a compilation of essential topics, questions to stimulate contemplation, and learning review questions to gauge your progression.

To ensure you stay on track and make progress, it's advised that you establish a timeline for completing the workbook. Set aside specific periods to work through the prompts and learning review questions. This will help you maintain your momentum and ensure you make steady progress.

The workbook commences with a short recap of the main book, acquainting you with the topic discussed in the title. This approach is highly beneficial for obtaining a deeper understanding of the content covered in the workbook, as well as identifying the areas that require the most attention.

The key lessons and the action prompts provided in this workbook aim to inspire contemplation on various facets of your life. You need not respond to all of them simultaneously and may revisit them later. They serve as a base for your self-reflection and personal exploration.

Once you complete the activities in this workbook, you can assess your progress by answering self-assessment questions. The purpose of these questions is to prompt you to reflect on your learning and identify which areas you need to focus on more. Armed with this knowledge, you can devise effective strategies to enhance your comprehension of the material.

Feel free to spend enough time on the prompts and self-assessment questions. You do not need to finish them in one go. You can take a pause and come back to them later. The most significant thing is to be truthful to yourself and to give careful thought to your responses.

Good luck!

Kelly Press

Overview

Trust is a book by Dr. Henry Cloud that explores the importance of trust in relationships and how to establish and maintain it. The book is divided into three parts, each focused on a different aspect of trust.

Part One, "Understanding Trust," explores the definition and components of trust. According to Cloud, trust consists of four components: character, competence, connection, and commitment. Each of these components is essential for trust to exist and thrive in a relationship. In this section, Cloud also explores the different types of trust, such as blind trust, situational trust, and earned trust, and how they affect relationships.

Part Two, "Building Trust," focuses on how to establish and maintain trust in relationships. Cloud provides practical advice on how to build trust by being honest, transparent, reliable, and empathetic. He also discusses the importance of boundaries, communication, and forgiveness in building and maintaining trust. This section also explores the role of trust in leadership and how leaders can earn the trust of their team members.

Part Three, "Rebuilding Trust," explores how to repair and restore trust when it has been broken. Cloud discusses the different levels of betrayal and how to approach repairing trust based on the severity of the breach. He provides practical strategies for rebuilding trust, such as acknowledging the hurt, taking responsibility, and making amends. This section also addresses the importance of self-trust and how to rebuild trust in oneself after a betrayal.

Throughout the book, Cloud uses real-life examples and case studies to illustrate his points and provide practical advice. He emphasizes the importance of trust in all types of relationships, from personal to professional, and provides readers with the tools they need to establish, maintain, and repair trust in their own lives.

In conclusion, Trust: Knowing When to Give It, When to Withhold It, How to Earn It, and How to Fix It When It Gets Broken is an insightful and practical guide to understanding and building trust in relationships. Cloud's approach is grounded in research and experience, making this book a valuable resource for anyone looking to improve their relationships and build stronger connections with others.

Trust Makes Life Work

Key Lessons

1. Trust is essential for healthy relationships: Trust is the foundation of all healthy relationships, and without it, relationships will struggle to survive. Trust is built on character, competence, connection, and commitment, and all of these elements must be present for trust to exist and thrive.

2. Boundaries are essential for building trust: Healthy boundaries are essential for building and maintaining trust in relationships. Clear boundaries help to establish expectations and guidelines for behavior, which can help prevent breaches of trust. Without boundaries, people are more likely to engage in behavior that can damage trust.

3. Transparency and honesty are crucial for building trust: Being transparent and honest is critical for building trust. People are more likely to trust someone who is open and honest about their intentions, actions, and feelings. Being transparent and honest can also help prevent misunderstandings and conflicts that can damage trust.

4. Trust takes time and effort to build: Trust is not built overnight, and it takes time and effort to establish and maintain. People must be willing to invest time and effort in building relationships, communicating openly and honestly, and showing that they are reliable and trustworthy.

5. Forgiveness is key to repairing broken trust: When trust is broken, forgiveness is key to repairing the relationship. Forgiveness involves letting go of resentment and anger, accepting responsibility for one's actions, and making amends. When both parties are willing to forgive and work towards rebuilding trust, relationships can become even stronger than before.

Action Prompts

How can you ensure that you are building relationships based on trust?

_____

_____

_____

_____

_____

_____

_____

_____

_____

_____

_____

_____

_____

What boundaries can you set to establish clear expectations and guidelines for behavior in your relationships?

_____

_____

_____

_____

_____

_____

_____

_____

_____

_____

_____

_____

_____

_____

How can you be more transparent and honest in your relationships to build trust?

_____

_____

_____

_____

_____

_____

_____

_____

_____

_____

_____

_____

_____

What steps can you take to invest time and effort into building and maintaining trust in your relationships?

_____

_____

_____

_____

_____

_____

_____

_____

_____

_____

_____

_____

_____

Have you ever experienced a breach of trust in a relationship? What steps did you take to repair the relationship?

_____

_____

_____

_____

_____

_____

_____

_____

_____

_____

_____

_____

_____

_____

How can you practice forgiveness in your relationships to repair broken trust?

_____

_____

_____

_____

_____

_____

_____

_____

_____

_____

_____

_____

What actions can you take to show that you are reliable
and trustworthy in your relationships?

_____

_____

_____

_____

_____

_____

_____

_____

_____

_____

_____

_____

How can you communicate openly and honestly with
others to build and maintain trust in your relationships?

_____

_____

The Five Essentials of Trust

Key Lessons

1. Start with yourself: Building trust starts with developing trust in yourself. You need to be trustworthy in order to earn the trust of others. This means being reliable, honest, and consistent.

2. Be transparent: Transparency is key to building trust. Be open and honest in your communication and actions. Avoid keeping secrets or hiding information that could affect others.

3. Practice empathy: Empathy is the ability to understand and share the feelings of others. It is an essential component of trust because it helps you connect with others on a deeper level. Show empathy by actively listening, understanding other people's perspectives, and showing concern for their feelings.

4. Keep your commitments: Keeping your commitments is a critical component of trust. If you make a promise, follow through on it. Be reliable and dependable. This will help others see you as trustworthy and dependable.

5. Set boundaries: Boundaries are essential for building and maintaining trust. They help you establish clear expectations and protect your own needs and values. Be clear about your boundaries and communicate them effectively to others. This will help them understand what you expect and how you want to be treated.

Action Prompts

How can you develop trust in yourself to be a trustworthy person?

_____

_____

_____

_____

_____

_____

_____

_____

_____

_____

_____

_____

_____

In what ways can you be more transparent in your communication and actions to build trust with others?

_____

_____

_____

_____

_____

_____

_____

_____

_____

_____

_____

_____

_____

_____

How can you practice empathy to better understand and connect with others and build trust?

_____

_____

_____

_____

_____

_____

_____

_____

_____

_____

_____

_____

_____

What steps can you take to ensure that you keep your commitments and build trust through reliability and dependability?

_____

_____

_____

_____

_____

_____

_____

_____

_____

_____

_____

_____

_____

How can you establish clear boundaries to protect your needs and values while building and maintaining trust with others?

_____

_____

_____

_____

_____

_____

_____

_____

_____

_____

_____

_____

_____

_____

What are some examples of situations where
transparency and honesty would be essential to build
trust?

_____

_____

_____

_____

_____

_____

_____

_____

_____

_____

_____

_____

_____

How can you actively listen to others and show concern
for their feelings to build trust and deeper connections?

_____

_____

_____

_____

_____

_____

_____

_____

_____

_____

_____

_____

_____

What are some effective ways to communicate your
boundaries to others and ensure they understand your
expectations for how you want to be treated?

Growing in Trust

Key Lessons

1. Honesty is the foundation of trust: To establish trust in a relationship, it is essential to be honest and transparent with the other person. This means being truthful about your feelings, intentions, and actions. Honesty is the foundation of trust and is necessary for building strong and meaningful connections with others.

2. Set and maintain healthy boundaries: Boundaries are essential for building and maintaining trust in relationships. Boundaries help establish a sense of safety and security, which is necessary for trust to thrive. It is important to set clear boundaries and communicate them effectively to the other person.

3. Communication is key: Communication is a crucial element in building and maintaining trust. It is essential to communicate openly, honestly, and effectively with the other person. This means actively listening to the other person and expressing your own thoughts and feelings in a clear and respectful manner.

4. Be reliable and consistent: Consistency is an important aspect of building trust in relationships. To establish trust, it is essential to be reliable and consistent in your actions and behavior. This means following through on your commitments, being dependable, and keeping your promises.

5. Forgiveness is necessary: Forgiveness is essential for repairing and restoring trust when it has been broken. It is important to acknowledge the hurt caused by the breach of trust, take responsibility for your actions, and make amends. Forgiveness allows for healing and the possibility of rebuilding trust in the relationship.

Action Prompts

How can you be more honest and transparent in your relationships to establish trust?

_____

_____

_____

_____

_____

_____

_____

_____

_____

_____

_____

_____

What healthy boundaries can you set and maintain to build and maintain trust in your relationships?

_____

_____

_____

_____

_____

_____

_____

_____

_____

_____

_____

_____

_____

_____

How can you improve your communication skills to better express yourself and actively listen to others to establish trust?

_____

_____

_____

_____

_____

_____

_____

_____

_____

_____

_____

_____

In what ways can you be more reliable and consistent in your actions and behavior to build trust in your relationships?

_____

_____

_____

_____

_____

_____

_____

_____

_____

_____

_____

_____

_____

How can you practice forgiveness when trust has been broken in a relationship to allow for healing and rebuilding?

_____

_____

_____

_____

_____

_____

_____

_____

_____

_____

_____

_____

What steps can you take to acknowledge the hurt caused by a breach of trust and take responsibility for your actions?

_____

_____

_____

_____

_____

_____

_____

_____

_____

_____

_____

_____

_____

_____

_____

How can you effectively communicate your commitments and keep your promises to establish trust with others?

_____

_____

_____

_____

_____

_____

_____

_____

_____

_____

_____

_____

_____

_____

In what ways can you prioritize the safety and security of others to establish trust in your relationships?

_____

_____

_____

_____

_____

_____

_____

_____

_____

_____

_____

_____

The Model for Repairing Trust

Key Lessons

1. Acknowledge the hurt: The first step in repairing trust is acknowledging the pain that has been caused. It is important to show empathy and understand the impact of the betrayal on the other person.

2. Take responsibility: The person who has broken the trust needs to take responsibility for their actions and the impact they have had on the relationship. This involves admitting fault and being accountable for their behavior.

3. Make amends: To repair trust, it is important to take action to make things right. This may involve making a sincere apology, offering restitution, or taking steps to prevent similar incidents from happening in the future.

4. Rebuild consistency: Rebuilding trust requires consistent behavior over time. This means following through on promises, being reliable, and communicating openly and honestly.

5. Have patience: Rebuilding trust takes time and patience. It may take months or even years to fully

restore trust in a relationship. It is important to stay committed to the process and not give up when progress is slow or difficult.

Action Prompts

Have you ever broken someone's trust? If so, have you acknowledged the hurt that you caused?

_____

_____

_____

_____

_____

_____

_____

_____

_____

_____

_____

_____

If you have broken someone's trust, did you take responsibility for your actions and the impact they had on the relationship?

_____

_____

_____

_____

_____

_____

_____

_____

_____

_____

_____

_____

_____

_____

What actions have you taken to make amends when you have broken someone's trust?

_____

_____

_____

_____

_____

_____

_____

_____

_____

_____

_____

_____

_____

_____

Have you ever experienced someone attempting to repair
trust with you? Did they make a sincere apology or offer
restitution?

_____

_____

_____

_____

_____

_____

_____

_____

_____

_____

_____

_____

_____

How consistent are you in following through on promises and being reliable? Do you think others see you as consistent and reliable?

_____

_____

_____

_____

_____

_____

_____

_____

_____

_____

_____

_____

Do you communicate openly and honestly with others, or do you tend to keep things to yourself?

_____

_____

_____

_____

_____

_____

_____

_____

_____

_____

_____

_____

_____

_____

_____

How patient are you when it comes to rebuilding trust? Do you tend to give up easily, or do you stay committed to the process?

_____

_____

_____

_____

_____

_____

_____

_____

_____

_____

_____

_____

_____

_____

If you have experienced a breach of trust in a relationship, what steps have you taken to repair it? Have you been patient with the process, or have you given up too quickly?

_____

_____

_____

_____

_____

_____

_____

_____

_____

_____

_____

_____

Moving Forward

Key Lessons

1. Take responsibility for the breach: The first step in rebuilding trust is to take responsibility for the breach. Cloud suggests that the person who broke the trust should take the initiative to repair it, regardless of who was at fault.

2. Acknowledge the hurt: It is important to acknowledge the hurt caused by the breach and to express empathy for the other person's feelings. This shows that you understand the impact of your actions and are willing to make things right.

3. Make amends: Making amends involves taking concrete steps to repair the damage caused by the breach. This may involve apologizing, offering restitution, or making changes to behavior that caused the breach in the first place.

4. Rebuild over time: Rebuilding trust takes time and effort. It involves consistently demonstrating trustworthiness through actions, not just words. Cloud suggests that it can take up to a year to rebuild trust in some cases.

5. Focus on self-trust: In addition to rebuilding trust with others, it is important to focus on rebuilding trust in oneself. This involves examining one's own values, beliefs, and behaviors and making changes as necessary to align them with one's own sense of integrity. Self-trust is essential for building and maintaining trust in relationships.

Action Prompts

When rebuilding trust, what steps can you take to demonstrate that you are taking responsibility for the breach?

_____

_____

_____

_____

_____

_____

_____

_____

_____

_____

_____

_____

_____

How can you acknowledge the hurt caused by a breach of trust and show empathy for the other person's feelings?

_____

_____

_____

_____

_____

_____

_____

_____

_____

_____

_____

_____

_____

_____

In what ways can you make amends when trust has been broken in a relationship?

_____

_____

_____

_____

_____

_____

_____

_____

_____

_____

_____

_____

_____

How long does it typically take to rebuild trust in a relationship, and what actions can you take to consistently demonstrate trustworthiness?

_____

_____

_____

_____

_____

_____

_____

_____

_____

_____

_____

_____

_____

Why is it important to focus on rebuilding trust in yourself in addition to rebuilding trust with others?

_____

_____

_____

_____

_____

_____

_____

_____

_____

_____

_____

_____

_____

What values, beliefs, and behaviors should you examine when focusing on rebuilding self-trust?

_____

_____

_____

_____

_____

_____

_____

_____

_____

_____

_____

_____

_____

_____

What changes can you make in your own life to align your values, beliefs, and behaviors with your sense of integrity?

_____

_____

_____

_____

_____

_____

_____

_____

_____

_____

_____

_____

_____

_____

How does rebuilding self-trust impact your ability to build and maintain trust in relationships with others?

_____

_____

_____

_____

_____

_____

_____

_____

_____

_____

_____

_____

_____

_____

Learning Review Questions

What made you purchase this workbook?

_____

_____

_____

_____

_____

_____

How have you been using the workbook so far?

_____

_____

_____

_____

_____

What do you feel you have gained from using the workbook?

_____

_____

_____

_____

_____

How has the workbook helped you to achieve your goals?

_____

_____

_____

_____

_____

_____

Are there any parts of the workbook that were particularly helpful or challenging for you?

_____

_____

_____

_____

_____

_____

How has your understanding or knowledge of the topic changed since working through the workbook?

_____

_____

_____

_____

_____

_____

_____

How do you plan to continue using the workbook or incorporating the information in your life?

_____

_____

_____

_____

_____

_____

_____